Mary in the Mystery

Mary in the Mystery

The Woman in Whom Divinity and Humanity Rhyme

Thomas J. Norris

Preface
by Stratford Caldecott

Afterword
by Léonie Caldecott

NEW CITY PRESS
Hyde Park, NY

Published in the United States by New City Press
202 Comforter Blvd., Hyde Park, NY 12538
www.newcitypress.com
© 2012 Thomas J. Norris

Cover design by Leandro de Leon

Library of Congress Cataloging-in-Publication Data:
Norris, Thomas J.
Mary in the mystery : the woman in whom divinity and humanity
rhyme /
Thomas J. Norris.
p. cm.
Includes bibliographical references (p.).
ISBN 978-1-56548-431-3 (pbk. : alk. paper)
1. Mary, Blessed Virgin, Saint--Theology. I. Title.
BT613.N67 2012
232.91--dc23
2011043076

Printed in the United States of America

Contents

Contents

Preface

A phrase from Dostoevsky's novel *The Idiot* often quoted out of context has almost taken on a life of its own: *Beauty will save the world*. It is a popular slogan because for many it seems to ring true; but it raises a question. Will the beauty that is in the world suffice to save it? Or must we look for a beauty from beyond the world? The answer is surely a bit of both. The beauty that is in the world comes from beyond it. The Christian religion is all about this saving beauty.

What is beauty? Beauty is that quality in a thing which attracts us towards itself, that in a sense *calls to us*. It calls us specifically "out of ourselves." The aesthetic experience is one of self-transcendence. Ugliness is imprisonment; beauty is a kind of liberation.

Goodness — for example moral goodness — is also beautiful, perhaps the best kind of beauty, spiritual beauty. For if being beautiful means being (potentially) admirable, or desirable, being *good* means to be *worthy* of being desired or admired. To judge something good or worthy of admiration is to think it right to admire this thing (as God did, when he made the world and "saw that it was good," in the first verses of the Book of Genesis). To assent in this way to a thing as beautiful is to receive it into myself, and not to reject it. It is to give the thing some kind of a home, to welcome it. For all things are naturally treated by the soul as gifts, coming from outside; and all beautiful things are recognizable as *good* gifts.

But as well as being beautiful and good, things also have a *meaning*. Whereas beauty refers to desirability, and goodness to worthiness, "truth" is the quality of a thing which gives it meaning. The precise degree of meaning in a thing depends on the kind of gift that it is. For example, something which "just happens" has no meaning beyond itself; but if it is a present from the person I love, the giver is in some way in the gift, and the *giver's love* is the meaning of the gift. A gift in this sense does not merely exist; it has a purpose, a reason; it makes sense, it has a "why." And we notice that in a loving gift, its truth, its goodness and its beauty are one. Love, in which one person expends him- or herself for another (for example, in courage or charity), is the most meaningful, the most desirable and the most worthy to be desired of all human experiences.

We can make sense of the world only by regarding the whole of existence as analogous to such a gift of love. The human experience of truth, goodness and beauty points us towards the Giver of the gift of being, the absolute Principle and Origin of all things. That reading of the world in the light of love is inspired and confirmed by the Christian revelation, which is the revelation of an absolute love at the very heart of the world.

"Our Lady"

And that is precisely why we need the kind of Mariology — that is, prayerful theological reflection on the Mother of God — that Tom Norris offers us in this booklet.

The eye of faith sees the invisible in the visible, and sees the visible world emerging from invisible depths. The Christian sees beauty, truth and goodness embodied in the man Jesus Christ. In him the invisible becomes visible; the visible is a sacrament of the invisible. But it is through Woman, through the Virgin called Mary, that this saving gift is given to the world. Mary is the world's representative creature, made beautiful by the gift of grace. She is the most beautiful of created persons, because she is the one who is fashioned by God to receive the gift of himself most worthily, on our behalf.

She is the heart of creation remade, rewoven, rebuilt as a Temple and a Palace, the shining and unbreakable core and foundation of a Church that is destined to become the home for all that is true, good and beautiful in the world.

It is in this Church (as the Russian thinker Nicolas Berdyaev wrote more succinctly than anyone else I have read) that "the grass grows and the flowers blossom, for the Church is nothing less than the cosmos Christianized."[1] Our Lady, the Virgin Mary, in the Catholic vision of things, is the beginning and mother of this Christian cosmos, this Christian people, and it is in her and in her children that the Church reveals herself to be more than merely the collection of flawed and sometimes corrupt human individuals that we see before us with our earthly eyes. This mystical and adamantine Church stands on the broad back of Peter and subsists in the Catholic Church *in the manner of a sacrament*.

The Catholic belief (confirmed by papal decree in 1854) that Mary was conceived immaculately, that is, without ever having been stained by Original Sin, is connected with this. The Church holds that the Virgin is blessed with perfect, unflawed freedom in the moment of her conception to ensure that her assent to the Incarnation is entirely her own act and no mere submission to an external force. Unless a new beginning had been made in her, she would have remained a member of the mystical body of Adam and implicated in his archetypal sin, unable fully to welcome the Word of God when he came to save us. Unless Mary had been free from sin from

---

1. *Freedom and the Spirit*, 331. The subsequent quotes are from p. 336.

the very beginning of her existence she would not have been the perfect receiver, both of Christ himself, and of the saving sacrifice that cannot be separated from his assumption of human nature.

The "Rhyming" of the Two Natures

Father Norris uses a beautiful expression to talk of Mary here. He says that in her womb the divine nature and the human nature, united in her Son, "rhyme" together. In poetry, the word "rhyme" refers to an echo or resemblance between two or more lines of the poem, particularly in the end of the lines — some way in which they sound alike whilst being different. The two natures of Christ, divine and human, are of course radically different. But in the Hypostatic Union the two natures converge on the same "end," the same "Word." This is divine poetry. The divine nature comes from heaven, and the human nature comes from Mary, like two kinds of music one above the other; they are "united without commingling," merging in one sound, one voice, one Gospel, one revelation.

Mary conceived Christ in her soul before she did so in her body. In her soul, then, this musical harmony resounds as it does in her womb. We hear the rhyme when she says to the Angel, "May it be done to me according to your word" (Lk 1:38). Mary has the soul of a poet, for the "business of the poets" (as G.K. Chesterton wrote in the introduction to his book on *Chaucer*) is to see all things in the "light of the positive" that distinguishes them from nothing, and to praise and give thanks for the deeds of their Creator — as Mary does in the *Magnificat*. Mary also has the soul of a theologian, for she treasures and ponders God's words and actions in her heart, drawing closer to her Son in spirit even as he has to distance himself from her physically. In our lecture halls and libraries we often forget that theology comes from Mary's home, and from the country roads where the first disciples heard a call to follow Jesus, and that its highest expression is the liturgy where we offer praise and thanks. Theology is at its most authentic when it is poetry and prayer, when it stammers and bleats and chants; not so much when it plods methodically through arguments and speculations.

The root of the word "rhyme" is the same as that of "rhythm" and even "arithmetic" — the word *arithmos* or *rim*, meaning "number" in Greek and Old English respectively, or *rythmos* referring to "measured motion." (Interestingly, the word for number may also be behind *ritus* or "religious custom.") Etymology is useful when, like this, it shows us connections we have forgotten. Fr. Norris speaks of the divine and the human "rhyme" as almost like a mathematical proportion, a cosmic harmony, thus reconnecting us with the Pythagoreans, for whom all things were made of numbers. Simone Weil saw ancient Greek geometry as "the most dazzling of all the prophecies which foretold the Christ,"[2] because it was all about the search for the mediation, or proportion, between two different numbers or lines (or sounds, in the case of musical harmony). In Mary the yearning for cosmic harmony felt by the ancient peoples, and expressed differently in the various civilizations, is fulfilled. The beauty revealed in her is "the completeness, the proportion and the *claritas*-radiance of divine revelation" itself, as Fr. Norris explains.

This essay on Mariology demonstrates a way of doing theology — a new way that is also an old way. We need continually to return to the springs of the tradition, where the life-giving waters flow still, as they flowed for the Church Fathers and still flow in abundance for the saints. The way to those springs leads back through the dry lands and mountains of academic theology, until we reach the simple human experience of a beauty that points us to the heart of our world and beyond the world.

---

2. Simone Weil, *Intimations of Christianity among the Ancient Greeks*, London 1957, 171.

What follows is an exercise in *poetic theology*, leading us into the mystery of Christ by exploring the wonderful harmony established in and through Mary between the divine and the human, united in the person of the Man who is also God — the Word, the Song, carried on the breath of God into the heart and womb of the Mother who loves him.

Stratford Caldecott

Introduction

Mary in the Mystery

Without Mariology, Christianity threatens imperceptibly to become inhuman. The Church becomes functionalistic, soulless, a hectic enterprise without any point of rest, made unfamiliar by the planners. And because, in this manly-masculine world, all that we have is one ideology replacing another, everything becomes polemical, critical, bitter, humorless, and ultimately boring, and people in their masses run away from such a Church.[1]

During the early part of Easter week in 1973, on the return trip from the Holy Land, I had the privilege of spending a few days in Istanbul, the city built by Constantine in the fourth century as the New Rome and the capital of the Eastern Empire. Located on the Bosporus where the Black Sea meets the Mediterranean Sea and Asia meets Europe, Istanbul was the venue for three of the early and decisive Ecumenical Councils of the Church. It was at these very Councils in fact that great truths of faith concerning Christ and the Trinity were unequivocally formulated for the People of God. The Church where these assemblies took place is the basilica of *Santa Sophia*. Almost inevitably, all tourists and visitors to the city will visit the basilica.

---

1. Hans Urs von Balthasar, *Elucidations*, London 1975, 72.

At the beginning of the second millennium, *Santa Sophia* witnessed the tragic schism between Constantinople and Rome, when Latin and Greek Christians separated in the fire of mutual recrimination and anathematization. Some four centuries later, Constantinople became a Muslim city. Finally, at the beginning of the last century, *Santa Sophia* was declared a state monument by a secular government. A prominently displayed sign announced a prohibition of prayer. Around me there were tourists with cameras and guide books accompanied by guides who explained the fascinating history of the great building. One of the guides pointed to an imposing mosaic of the Virgin and Child high in the cupola, with the Mother of God offering the Child. The mosaic had not been covered over in the vicissitudes of the great basilica's history.

Santa Sophia and its almost two-thousand year history are a witness and a parable, as it were. It witnesses to the sequence of the original unity of Christians, their lacerated unity, the arrival of another faith, and, finally, the removal of all religion and its replacement by a view of life and history that leaves out all religion. The presence of the *Theotokos* and Child, however, is a comfort. And a lesson: her mosaic often sets in motion a train of thought. Christ is a gift, the greatest in fact. God cannot be imposed. The Gospel cannot be forced upon anyone, though its core is so splendid and its message corresponds to the intrinsic nostalgia for the divine that inhabits human hearts. The good news of Christ can only be offered, since Faith is a gift, and faith-life the effect of freely given grace. The best way to offer it, in point of fact, is to witness with one's life, as the *Theotokos* did.

Simple Yet Radical

The mosaic of the Virgin and Child focused my reflection further. Mary seemed to be saying something quite simple and, at the same time, quite radical: namely, in order to give Christ to men and women it is first necessary for Christ to be in us and for us to be in Christ. No one gives what one does not have. When one of those early Ecumenical Councils (in fact the third, which was held at Ephesus in the year 431) had solemnly declared Mary to be the *Theotokos*, or the *Genetrix* of God, it was saying that a mere creature had, through the grace of the God of Abraham, begotten in our human flesh and for humankind the very God who had "created the heavens and the earth" (Gen 1:1). An unassuming servant of God had done the greatest of all deeds: she had facilitated the Son of the Eternal becoming present on earth in our own flesh and blood. In the words of the nineteenth century Jesuit and poet, Gerard Manley Hopkins, she

> *Gave God's infinity*
> *Dwindled to infancy*
> *Welcome in womb and breast.*

> *[Mary] this one work has to do —*
> *Let all God's glory through,*
> *God's glory which would go*
> *Through her and from her flow*
> *Off, and no way but so.*[2]

Christians, I began to think, need to be not only Christ-like but also Mary-like, indeed "other Marys," so that God can live among his people and find welcome from them (cf. Is 7:14; Mt 1:23; Jn 1:11–13; 14:23). No amount of Christian history, no teaching, however wonderful and attractive in itself, no artistic expression of the sublime, can root the divine in our world and in human hearts without an earlier and more vital fact being in place: the handing over to God of all our mind, and all our strength, and all our heart, so that he can re-enter the world which he "re-created" in and through our human flesh.

In what follows, we will attempt in the first instance to present the scripturally honed "figure" of Mary[3] in order to situate her within the mystery of Christ, "that mystery which affects

---

2. Gerard Manley Hopkins, "The Blessed Virgin Compared to the Air We Breathe," in *Poems and Prose*, London 1986, 55.

3. See *Lumen Gentium*, 55.

the whole history of the human race, influences the Church continuously, and is principally exercised by the priestly ministry."[4] To do so we will situate Mary along the horizon of the world religions and in the context of the salvation history that unfolds between Abraham and the God of Israel down the long centuries of the Old Testament. This will enable us to ponder Mary's unique encounter with the Christian Mystery. In Mary one may glimpse the fullness (*pleroma*) of the Mystery of Christ:

> *And her hand leaves his light*
> *Sifted to suit our sight.*[5]

In the second place, we will direct our attention to the adventure of Mary, her own unique spiritual journey. St. Luke highlights what people today call spirituality. Twice in the space of one chapter, he tells us that Mary "treasured all these things" and that "she pondered them in her heart" (2:18; 51). Mary is clothed in the Word of God given to the patriarchs and the prophets. In that way she is prepared and disposed for the Word of whom St. John writes at the very outset of his Gospel,

> In the beginning was the Word,
> And the Word was with God,

---

4. Second Vatican Council, *Optatam Totius* (Decree on Priestly Formation), 14. *Lumen Gentium* is the Dogmatic Constitution on the Church produced a year earlier by the Council in 1964.

5. Hopkins, *ibid.*

And the Word was God ...
All things were made through him.

Mary is the Woman of the Scriptures, as
St. John suggests on two occasions in his Gospel (2:4; 19:26). She is actually clothed with the
Word of the God of Israel who is also the God
of all the nations. In that way, Mary is enabled
to represent her own people, Israel, in the final
dialogue of life between the God of Abraham,
Isaac and Jacob, and the human family. She is
convinced that the God of Abraham remem-
bers his mercy for Israel and for the whole of
humanity. Such representation, of course, can
only take place by divine appointment. And
this is precisely what happens in the annunciation (Lk 1:26–38) in the home of Nazareth.

There she encounters, representatively for
the whole human family, the mystery of God who
is Love. St. Luke's account delicately mentions
the gift of "the Son of the Most High" and the
"overshadowing of the Holy Spirit" (1:32, 35).
The blessed Trinity, in a word, becomes the very
setting, the milieu, of Mary's life. She will follow
that in-breaking Love into the long night of
suffering all the way to the Cross where, decades
later, the prophecy of Simeon is fulfilled (cf.
2:25–32). There at the foot of the Cross she will
receive in pain and joy a second motherhood,
that of the members of her Son, the Church,

before the dawn of the new day of Pentecost (cf. Jn 19:25–27).

In the third place, there is Mary's entry into the mission of Christ and his Church. As the completely redeemed and assumed Virgin-Mother of God, her role is that of a maternal intercession above and a constant "mothering" below. In that way she "takes part in the life of the Church" (Pope Paul VI) and helps to form children who are true "copies" of her divine Son (cf. Jn 19:27), as Origen of Alexandria already perceived in the third century.[6] Here we will perceive the radiant light she radiates out over the total mission of the Church. Finally, there is our call to set out on the holy journey and adventure which Mary has so vividly illuminated. The true glory of Christians is to relive the adventure of Mary, all due proportion being safeguarded.

6. Origen, *Commentary on John* 1, 6: PG 14, 32.

Chapter I

Mary's Place in the Mystery: Fullness

In order to "realize" the mystery of Christ it is first necessary to situate him in the context of humankind's great search. That search is the golden thread running through our religious history. It expresses itself in terms of those questions that are ineradicable from the human heart. In fact, in the encyclical *Fides et Ratio*, Pope John Paul II stresses that it is possible to read in the register of religions, beginning with the most ancient, the search for the answers to the questions that will never leave the human mind and heart.[1] Quoting the Council's *Decree on the Church's Relation to the Great Religions*, he writes,

> People look to the various religions for answers to those profound mysteries of the human condition which, today, even as in olden times, deeply stir the human heart: What is a human being? What is the meaning and purpose of our life? What is goodness and what is sin? What gives rise to our sorrows, and to what intent? Where lies the path to true happiness? What is the truth about death, judgement and retribution beyond the grave? What, finally, is that ultimate and unutterable mystery which engulfs our being, and from which we take our origin and towards which we move?[2]

---

1. Pope John Paul II, *Fides et Ratio*, 2.
2. Second Vatican Council, *Nostra Aetate*, 2.

These are the fundamental and definitive questions which most occupy the human family. All religions, in fact, attempt to address these concerns.

The Ancient Cultures

In the ancient cultures, four elements or "components" of reality were evaluated as if in solidarity with each other. These components were *the divine, the human being, society* and *the cosmos*. All ancient cultures gave precedence to the solidarity of these components over their differentiation. They stressed what some have called their "consubstantiality." Authors speak accordingly of the "cosmological cultures" where the Divine was perceived as the all-embracing layer of the world. In these the Divine was co-extensive with all the layers of reality, effectively penetrating into all of them. The result was a kind of "compact consciousness."[3] The sting of mortality, however, made human beings aware of the more lasting components of the cosmos. Thus the family lasted longer than any particular family member, the clan outlasted the family, while the hills and the planets outlasted them all. The result was that human beings sought to attune themselves to the more lasting components

---

3. See Eric Voegelin, *Order and History*, volumes I–IV, being volumes XIV–XVII of the *Collected Works*, Columbia, MO.

of reality. This is the key to myth, which is the earliest attempt to symbolize the order of reality in a meaningful drama.

With the differentiation of consciousness, however, there came the emergence of the ancient religions. As glorious "spiritual outbursts" (Eric Voegelin), the Great Religions differentiate the divine from the components of the cosmos. This is what occurs with both the great religions of Asia and with philosophy in ancient Greece. The divine is put outside the cosmos, and can be reached only by a heroic journey of the soul. The world, the other, and society are to be left behind, since they are not the divine Ground. The whole plethora of mythological cosmology, Asiatic religions and Greek philosophy consists in a search "from below," as it were. At most, they can find the "One," the "First" and the "Last," the "Ground" and "Cause" of the many components of the universe. However, this "One" is perceived as impersonal, a Being without a face — like the Unmoved Mover of Aristotle.

Called Out of Egypt

This is the necessary historical and theological context for understanding *revealed religion*. Revealed religion is the religion that God gives. It results from the divine initiative taken with Abraham and his children who become the nation

of Israel. This nation gradually realizes that it is
the Beyond who has initiated the search for them.
The living God is seeking them out! The Prophets
stress the fact even further. In the eighth century
B.C., the Prophet Hosea proclaims, "When Israel
was a child, I loved him, and I called my son out
of Egypt" (Hos 11:1). The unfolding drama of this
revelation to the children of Abraham discloses
the true meaning of all the components of reality.
Thus the divine, the human, society and the world
are now under a new light, the light of revelation.
It is that light which unfolds their meaning. The
Divine becomes the personal God who speaks to
the patriarchs and manifests himself as the God
of Abraham and Isaac and Jacob: the history of
what he will do with this people will become the
very key to his being, just as the deeds of any
person reveal his or her character. History, then,
will become increasingly the key to divinity.

The human being for his part is made "in the
image and likeness of this God" (Gen 1:26–27).
He is, if you like, a "You" for God. As addressed
by the creative word of God, he is a hearer of
that creative and transforming *dabar*. This is the
ultimate truth about the human being: he is a
potential hearer of the Word of the living and
acting God. And what of human society? The society of Israel is a People chosen and called to be
the witnesses to God's reality and truth among,

and even to, the nations. Finally, the world and the cosmos are "the good creation" of God and speak his glory with eloquence.

And still the fulfillment of this dialogue of two "partners" lies in the future. With the passing of the centuries, Israel realizes ever more deeply her incapacity to live consistently in the divine milieu opened up by the Covenant. Only fresh and ever more radical divine interventions can sustain the Covenant through time. The God of Abraham, Isaac and Jacob orientates her towards a definitive future which can only be ushered in by a unique adventure — the arrival of the Messiah. This fact will constitute both the drama and the glory of Israel. However, it situates the center of gravity of Israel's drama in the future.

God's Final Move

Mary of Nazareth is to be theologically situated in Israel and at the point where God makes his final move. The revelation of the First Covenant constitutes both the historical and the theological key to her person and her place in the events of the New Covenant. Accordingly, it is important to see in her a daughter of Abraham, a beneficiary of the Covenant and, like all the prophets, someone looking forward to the "new thing" (Is 40:3) and "the comforting of Israel" (Lk 2:25). She will be there when "the glory of her people Israel" and "the light to enlighten the Gentiles" (Lk 2:32) promised by the prophets will shine out. St. Augustine saw Mary, in fact, as conceiving Christ in her mind even before she conceived him in her womb.[4]

In the fullness of time, however, there came the fullness of revelation (Gal 4:4–7). The four partners in the Great Dialogue are linked in a mysterious and profound fashion. In fact, God's dialogue with humankind now becomes union. The eternal Word of God who *is* God crosses the abyss separating divinity and humanity. The result is, in the words of T. S. Eliot, "Incarnation. Here the impossible union of spheres of existence is actual."[5] The Word becomes flesh, taking on our human nature and our human condition, truly "flesh of our flesh." The Son is "born of woman" (Gal 4:4). As for the People of Israel, they become the "Body of Christ," a body universal in space and in time where everyone is, or is called to be, a son/daughter of the Father, a sister/brother of Christ, and a temple of their Holy Spirit. A new humanity is born (2 Cor 5:17; Gal 6:15). As for creation, it is resurrected with Christ and groans with the birth pangs of the "new creation" (Rom 8:19–23).

The mystery of Christ thus opens a future of

---

4. St. Augustine, *Sermo* 25, 7–8.

5. T. S. Eliot, *The Four Quartets, Dry Salvages,* V.

promise and hope for all creation. That mystery engages the great thinkers of the early Church. One of the earliest and greatest was St. Irenaeus of Lyons, who suffered martyrdom around 210 A.D. As if looking back over the whole panorama of the history of salvation, he writes these words, "God is the glory of man. However, man exists in order to be the receptacle of the action of God as well as of all his wisdom and power."[6] This God is unlimited in his goodness. The reason for this divine generosity is well expressed by Dionysius the Areopagite and St. Thomas Aquinas, "Goodness loves to give itself away."[7]

Now in that wondrous linking of the components of reality, a woman plays an incomparable role. If we are to appreciate what she is to be in the new and eternal Covenant, it is important to appreciate what she *already* is in the Mosaic Covenant. Her God is the Lord God of Israel, whom she will soon praise in the *Magnificat* that has continued to resonate down the arches of the centuries. He is the God revealed through the ages of Israel and the vicissitudes of Israel's history. That history is the story of a mercy and love that enlarge in proportion as the need for them increases. As for herself, she knows that

---

6. St. Irenaeus, *Adversus Haereses*, Bk. III, 20, 2: *Sources Chretiennes* 34, 342.

7. St. Thomas, *Summa*, III, q.1, a.1.

she is a "You" before that same God, being
made in his very image and likeness. She
realizes, accordingly, that the God of her people
desires relationship with her, and she for her
part grows in the desire to reciprocate that
very relationship. As for her nation, the Chosen
People, she senses poignantly the predicament
of her brothers and sisters. God is near them
indeed, and yet his definitive Deed in their
favor is placed firmly in the future, at a time
which he will decide. In her soul, there is the
desire to correspond with all her being to the
"design of God which lasts forever" (Ps 33:11),
whatever it may be and however it may overtax
her resources. As for God's good creation, it
reveals to her externally the glory of the God
she already perceives within.

A Profile of the Woman

In fact, the inspired Word of the Old
Testament already provided a profile and heuristic
of the woman who would be associated with the
Messiah. For down the ages of the Old Testament,
"the figure of a woman, mother of the Redeemer,"
as *Lumen Gentium* teaches, is brought into "a
gradually clearer light."[8] This woman will be the
particular instrument of God and a key player

---

8. *Lumen Gentium*, 55.

at the zero hour of his dealings with his People, and through them with the whole human family. However, the sketch is drawn slowly. Certain authors have highlighted the decisive lines in the sketch.[9] It is important to mention them briefly here as we build up the first testament's "identikit" of the woman who was destined to be the associate of Israel's Messiah.

First, there is the "Woman" of Genesis. She is the equal partner of Adam, being made in the image and likeness of God in equal fashion with him. As mother of all the living, she is the guardian of the gift of life, the one "original blessing" not forfeited in the Fall. It is not good for man to be without her, and so she is created as the gift that takes him out of his "original solitude" (cf. Gen 1–2). She is an "I" in the same nature as man, who is intended to be a "You" for her.[10]

The second line in the sketch is that of the "Unblessed-blessed Mothers" in the Old Covenant. These include Sarah, the wife of Abraham, Rebekah, the wife of Isaac, and Hannah, the wife of Elkanah and mother of Samuel (Gen 12:5; 25:19–28; 1 Sam 1). Though barren by nature, each became a mother through the gracious mercy

---

9. For example, Joseph Ratzinger, *Daughter Zion*, San Francisco 1987.

10. See Klaus Westermann, "Genesis 1–11," in *Genesis,* vol. 1 of *Biblischer Kommentar, Altes Testament,* Neukirchen 1974.

of God. And not only a mother: the child born each time became a vital connection in the history-making and unfolding design of God. Isaac is born to Abraham and Sarah as a blessing-gift of God in order to initiate the fulfillment of God's promise to Abraham — the promise to make his descendants as numerous as the sand on the seashore and the stars in the sky. From Rebekah is born Jacob, whose twelve sons become the fathers of the twelve tribes of Israel. As for Hannah's son, Samuel, his ministry at the beginning of the eleventh century B.C. occurs at a most delicate time in the history of Israel. From Sarah to Elizabeth there runs a straight line: its message is that God brings about his greatest works on the background of our human insufficiency, like a painting against its black background. "My grace is enough for you: my power is at its best in weakness" (2 Cor 12:9). In these women there is a sustained revelation of a theology of the Covenant in the very pattern of the unblessed becoming the blessed mothers of key figures in salvation history.

A third line in the sketch is provided in the post-exilic theology of the Daughter of Zion (Zeph 3:14–18). This is a representative figure who sums up Israel before the God of the Covenant. God will enlist her co-operation to fulfill his plan for his beloved people.

The Woman of the Scriptures

By putting these three strands together, one arrives at a dynamic theology of Israel as God's bridal people. Above all, though, one sets the stage for the woman of the Scriptures, the virgin Mary of Nazareth and her unique role when, in "the fullness of time" there occurred "the fullness of revelation" in Christ. As the Son of the Father in heaven the eternal Word now becomes the Son of Mary on earth. He "is both the sum total and the mediator of all revelation."[11]

St. Luke's account of the incarnation combines simplicity with subtlety.[12] He perceives that "in Mary, Zion passes over into the Church; in her, the Word passes over into flesh; in her, the Head passes over into the body. She is the place of superabundant fruitfulness."[13] He highlights the self-communication of the God of Israel in his Son and by the Holy Spirit, on the one hand, and Mary welcoming this revelation, on the other. Luke, in other words, opens up for his readers the mystery-wonder of what happened at this extraordinary moment when God offers his Son to humankind represented by the person of the

---

11. *Dei Verbum*, 2.

12. See Ignace de la Potterie, *Mary in the Mystery of the Covenant*, New York 1992; René Laurentin, *The Truth of Christmas beyond the Myths*, Pertersham, Massachussetts 1986.

13. Hans Urs von Balthasar, *The Glory of the Lord*, I, Edinburgh 1982, 338.

virgin of Nazareth, and she for her part conceived him by the overshadowing of the Holy Spirit. This will be Luke's theological lesson, as it were.

However, as an historian of salvation, which is his favorite perspective, Luke locates Mary at the point where the Old Covenant passes over into the New and Eternal Covenant, the synagogue becomes the Church, and God becomes man in order "to reign over the house of Jacob forever" in a "kingdom that will have no end" (Lk 1:33).[14] In and through the mystery of Christ, *and never simply in parallel to that mystery*, Mary will highlight the new identity of God, of the human being, of mankind and of creation.[15] She can do this because

> her centrality is radically relational.... She is that center in which the Blessed Trinity and humankind encounter in an embrace that becomes indissoluble. Her design is that of "being by not being" so that this encounter could happen. In that sense she is "humble and high" more than any other creature (Dante Alighieri).[16]

---

14. See Hans Urs von Balthasar, *Theo-Drama*, III, San Francisco 1992, 328–334.

15. See Thomas J. Norris, "Mariology a Key to the Faith," in *Irish Theological Quarterly*, 55(1989), 193–205.

16. Piero Coda, "Imparare la vita trinitaria guardando a Maria" in Giuseppe Greco (ed.), *Il pianto di Maria*, Rome 2003, 256, quoting Dante's *La divina commedia*, Il Paradiso, Canto XXXIII.

Mary becomes an "explanation" of God and a gradually ascending plane to his mystery.[17]

St. Luke's annunciation story is the account of a conception and of a vocation. There is the conception of the eternal Son by the overshadowing of the Holy Spirit, and there is the vocation of Mary to welcome and co-operate with the gift of the God of Abraham, Isaac and Jacob.[18] Mary's is therefore a new experience of the God of her fathers, the experience in fact of an utterly new in-breaking of the God of Israel into her personal history. God has an eternal Son, and that Son is being offered to Mary to be born of her own flesh and blood! Mary for her part is being called and invited to become the Mother of God's Son by the overshadowing of the Holy Spirit. Luke describes a God who is a dynamic and "organic" Trinity: the God who gives, the God who is Son (and wishes to become Son of a creature on earth), and the God who as the Holy Spirit will bring this about. Mary experiences in her total humanity of spirit, soul and body-flesh the irruption of the divine Trinity into the history of her people. To quote a rhetorical question from Pope John Paul's remarkable Apostolic Letter, *On the Dignity of Women*, "Do we not find in the Annunciation at Nazareth the beginning of that

---

17. See Chiara Lubich, *Meditations*, London 2005, 116–118.
18. See Ignace de la Potterie, *ibid*., 3–35.

definitive answer by which *God himself 'attempts to calm people's hearts'*?"[19]

The dialogue genre of the annunciation story masterfully serves to underline the revelation occurring therein. The first part of the dialogue points us towards Mary's election by the Lord (v. 28b). The content of this election is the coming of "the Son of the Most High" (32), whom Mary is called to conceive and bear. Such a wonder as the conception of a pre-existing Son by a creature causes perplexity and fear, the inevitable *shaking of the foundations* at the approach of divine infinity (28b–30). Mary formulates the inevitable question: How can something so utterly unprecedented happen at all (34)? The angel introduces the Holy Spirit. He will accomplish the enfleshing of the eternal Son in Mary. Here is the first revelation of what theology will later call the "economic" Trinity (the Trinity in history and making history). This revelation precedes by thirty years its gradual manifestation to the Twelve in the ministry, paschal mystery and glorification of Jesus as Lord and Savior. Mary is truly *Rúnaí Dé* (in Gaelic, "the Secretary of God"), the Keeper of the Secrets of God.

Luke's dialogue skillfully manifests the mystery of the self-communication of God the

---

19. Pope John Paul II, Apostolic Letter *Mulieris Dignitatem*, 1988, no. 3.

Holy Trinity to Mary and humankind. However, it highlights with incomparable skill the personal role of Mary in synergy with that of the Holy Spirit.[20] St. Bernard of Clairvaux has noticed this dimension and described it in a text that touchingly captures the role of Mary, setting it in the context of the history of salvation.

> The angel is waiting for your answer: it is time for him to return to God who sent him.... In the eternal Word of God were we all made, and lo! we die; by one little word of yours in answer shall all be made alive.... Arise, then, run and open. Arise by faith, run by devotion of your heart, open by your word.[21]

It was St. Thomas Aquinas who famously affirmed that Mary of Nazareth responded to the God of Israel "in the place of the whole of human nature."[22] Her experience of divine revelation as

---

20. Piero Coda sees "the evangelist highlighting the distinct but marvelously synergic role of the Holy Spirit and of Mary in the realization of this event," *op. cit.*, 258.

21. St. Bernard, *Homilies in Praise of the Virgin Mother*, Hom 4, 8–9 as translated in *The Divine Office*, I, Dublin 1974, 141–142. The Anglican theologian, A. M. Allchin, has noted how "Gregory Palamas, the greatest theologian of the later Middle Ages in the Christian east, speaks of our Lady as being herself the *methorion*, the threshold, the boundary between earth and heaven," *The Joy of All Creation*, London 1993, 144–145.

22. St. Thomas, *Summa*, III, q.30, a.1: *Per annuntiationem expectebatur consensus Virginis loco totius humanae naturae.* ("By means of the annunciation the consent of the Virgin was desired in the place of the whole human race.")

the self-communication of God the Holy Trinity
is therefore earlier, greater and more original than
that of the Twelve and the apostolic Church.

In the Acts of the Apostles, his second
volume describing the emergence of the Church
as a people shaped by and living from the life
given by God the Holy Trinity, Luke places
Mary in the very first scene. Since the Church is
the event of Christ spreading out in space and
in time, this spreading will always require the
maternal presence of the *Theotokos*. In any case,
Luke situates her among the Eleven,[23] "certain
women" and "his brothers" (1:14). They await in
prayer the promised Holy Spirit (cf. Lk 24:49). The
promise made by Jesus to the Apostles before his
ascension, that they "will receive power when the
Holy Spirit comes upon" them (Acts 1:8), brings
to mind the angel's promise to Mary of the gift
of the Holy Spirit as the agent of the incarnation
of the Son (Lk 1:35). As the Holy Spirit and Mary
co-operated synergically in the incarnation of the
Son thirty-three years earlier, so now they will co-
operate again in the "incarnation" of her Son in the
community of the Church. Mary's motherhood is
thereby extended into the mystery of the Church,
as that part of humankind that lives from and in

---

23. Could it be that this is a hint at the complementarity between
the New Eve and the Petrine Church, which is now under seri-
ous challenge?

her divine Son. Being identified with the event of
Christ becoming incarnate in humankind to the
end of time, the Church can never arrive at the
moment when she would no longer need the Holy
Spirit and Mary. As the Second Vatican Council
teaches, Mary "co-operates with a mother's love
in the generation and formation of the faithful."[24]

A New Identity

Who, then, is Mary? Following the revelation in
the first Covenant, Mary is to be found in a new set
of relationships. These relationships have emerged
in the unique event of the annunciation, conception
and birth of the Son in her flesh, which had united
God, humanity, society and the world into the
drama of the new Covenant (Lk 22:20; 1 Cor 11:25).
They now sing out her fresh identity, and with that
what we too are to become, our new human vocation. In Mary we see that God is the Father who
gave his Son and poured out his Holy Spirit, the
"sign of the new creation" (Gen 1:2). Mary is the
elected daughter of that Father, the Mother of his
eternal Son and the dwelling place (*shekinah*) of the
Holy Spirit. Her identity is completely relational,
since her whereabouts is radically Trinitarian as
the chosen daughter of the Father, the mother of
his Son and the temple of their Holy Spirit.

---

24. *Lumen Gentium*, 63.

As to how she sees herself, Mary has a new identity, a new "I" that is utterly transformed. She had always escaped the snare of being self-absorbed or self-contemplative. She could never see herself as a personality, but only as the Lord's "lowly handmaid" and servant (Lk 1:36, 48). Her very humility has drawn down the affection and philanthropy (Tit 2:11) of God from heaven to earth. Charles Péguy stresses that she is the one created being who is entirely pure and yet entirely fleshly. She is

> infinitely pure because infinitely poor, infinitely exalted because infinitely humbled, infinitely young because infinitely maternal, infinitely upright because infinitely inclined in mercy, infinitely joyful because infinitely sorrowful.[25]

Identified in the annunciation as an utterly unique "You" for the God and Father of Jesus Christ, in fact as the "one transformed by grace" (cf. Lk 1:28, 30), Mary welcomes the divine *ouverture* as the arms of the Father (St. Irenaeus) stretch out and embrace her as the representative of Israel and humanity.

As the most graced of creatures, she now begins to live by the relations that constitute the mystery of the Blessed Trinity. She begins to

---

25. Charles Péguy, *Oeuvres poetiques completes*, Paris 1941, 206.

show and to teach the new life that is given from above. Now the lesson of salvation history is that *what comes down from heaven must also grow up from the earth.*[26] Mary shows it to us so that we may look upon the Trinitarian life (1 Jn 1:2), gradually learn it, and perhaps approximate a little to what happened to us in Baptism, and to what we profess when we pray the Liturgy. If, as Paul instructs his converts in Colossae, the lives of believers "are hidden with Christ in God" (Col 3:3), then Mary is the archetype of such surprising location. In the words of Klaus Hemmerle,

> Mary is in the garden of the Trinity, guarded by the Father above her who loves her, by the Son within her and in the neighbor, and by the Spirit who forms the new "We," the new people of God.[27]

As for her "society," it is that of the Church, the people the Fathers of the Church loved to describe as being "made one by the unity of the Father, the Son and the Holy Spirit."[28] This people, growing in history from the time of Abel

---

26. Klaus Hemmerle, *Brücken zum Credo*, Freiburg im Breisgau 1984, 18–20.

27. Idem, *Partire dall'unità*, Rome 1995, 131 (translation my own).

28. St. Cyprian, *De oratione dominica*, 23: PL 4, 553; St. Augustine, *Sermo* 71, 20; 33: PL 38, 463f; St. John Damascene, *Adversus Iconocl.*, 12: PG 96, 1358D; text quoted in *Lumen Gentium*, 4.

the just, and destined to grow until the end of
time, is now "the Israel of God" (Gal 6:16) and
the beloved Bride of the Lamb (Rev 21). All the
generations of this people will call Mary blessed
(cf. Lk 1:48). As for Mary, each member of the
New Society is a replica-image of her firstborn
Son (Lk 2:7) and therefore a beloved brother or
sister, as well as a child (Jn 19:27). The reason for
this is that each is a sacrament of the enfleshed
Son of her womb. With her transformed "I,"
Mary sets out to help and accompany her ageing
cousin, Elizabeth (Lk 1:37). She will always have
eyes for the practical needs of those around her
as the wedding episode at Cana will further
show (Jn 2:1–5).

Finally, there is the world of creation where
Mary is a "culmination of evolution, heaven-
sent revolution."[29] As the "wild web, wondrous
robe" who "mantles the guilty globe,"[30] Mary is
creation *as it was in the beginning.* She is Paradise
Regained, or, in the words of William Wordsworth, "our tainted nature's solitary boast."[31]
Since she is creation in full bloom, the fruit had
to be Jesus, the most beautiful of the children of
men. In Mary creation has an immaculate core or

---

29. I am indebted for this idea to Susan Gately.
30. Hopkins, *ibid.,* 55.
31. William Wordsworth, *Sonnet to Our Lady;* see A. M. Allchin, *The
    Joy of all Creation,* 141f.

heart: it is good through and through as on the seventh day of creation (Gen 1:31). This is in part what is meant by saying that she was conceived immaculately.

Mary, then, is the witness to the fullness of the Christian Mystery. Since that mystery brings together God, humanity, society and world, the components of reality, without confusion and without separation, and since Mary is situated by the Father's most wise design at the axis of so great an event, she is an exceptional witness to the mystery. That mystery, however, generates communion between earth and heaven. Into that communion humanity is called. To it we now turn in order to discern the way Mary enables us to understand and, in particular, to live in and for this communion.

Chapter II

Mary in the Communion of the Church:
Harmony and Proportion

The place of Mary in the mystery of Christ already defines her place in the communion of the Church. That communion flows from the revealed mystery that had fascinated St. Paul (Rom 16:26; 1 Cor 2:7; 10:16–17; Eph 3:10; Col 2:2–3). It does so every bit as naturally as a river cascades down the wooded valleys from its source in the mountains.

Mary co-operates in forming the communion of the Church. What does this mean? Simply that she is the woman through whom the eternal communion of the Trinity has opened out to the world in and through the economy of her divine Son *but never beside him*. She lives the implications of this fact in her own faith journey. Her journey illuminates our own journey, and "X-rays" the human condition, as it were. Her witness to communion is captured in the four Marian dogmas that highlight her place and point towards ours in "the Church that is born from the Trinity."[1] She invites us to go on that holy journey, believing that love and loving are the strongest forces in the universe, even as she shows us how to travel through those great realms which divine revelation opens up for the lost children of the First Eve. This twofold com-

---

1. Henri de Lubac, "Ecclesia de Trinitate" in *The Motherhood of the Church*, San Francisco 1982, 113–140.

munion is vitally important for the light which it will throw upon the basic form or shape of the Christian life and way.

One needs to stress the danger of a Mary who is removed from our human condition, a Mary with whom modern men and women could not identify. Such a Mariology, however, would already misrepresent the woman who saw the shadow of the cross overshadowing her from the beginning of her own journey of faith (Lk 1:35), and who could never forget what Simeon, representing Israel in its mode of prophecy, had foretold as "the sword of sorrow" hanging over her like the sword of Damocles. The lance and the cross will await her and her Son at the appointed "hour" (Jn 2:4; 19:25–2). She is, after all, someone blessed because she believed (Lk 1:45), someone whose faith is challenged at key moments in her Son's journey when she does not understand (Lk 2:33, 48; Jn 2:4), and someone who will live the forsakenness of her Son on Calvary in a representative capacity (Jn 19:25–8).

In following her journey as a woman of communion as outlined in the Scriptures, we will be studying the Mother of Jesus existentially. We will see that Mary is the "woman of the Word," who accompanies, as no other ever has, her Son in his Paschal Mystery before receiving a unique and maternal mediation. In the second instance, studying the dogmas of faith that tell us who she is and what we are to become with her, we will perceive how we are together embedded in the realms of reality disclosed in divine revelation. She will help us appreciate, individually and collectively, some of the unfathomable riches of her Son, his free gifts to us (Eph 3:8), and the greatness of the love with which he has loved us (Eph 2:4). Perhaps wonder will return, that fountainhead of all learning, knowledge and spiritual achievement, and only effective antidote to the cynicism and surrender that are the besetting temptations of believers in this as in all ages. After all, "anyone who does not welcome the kingdom of God like a little child will never enter it" (Lk 18:17).

A "Double Incarnation" of the Word

The Mary of the New Testament is the greatest hearer and "doer of the Word" (Jas 1:22). She stands before the God of Israel with an attitude of total readiness. Such readiness corresponds to her role as the Daughter of Zion who represents the Israel of God. The Word of that God cannot go forth without accomplishing what it is meant to do (Is 55:10–11). That Word, however, also dialogues with each intended hearer, as the whole of the Old Testament stresses. In the Annunciation event, Mary hears that Word so deeply and elects it so radically that the Word becomes flesh of her flesh and bone of her bone. She could not incarnate the Word of herself: "How can this be since I am a virgin?" (Lk 1:34). Her virginity manifests vividly this very incapacity, as Karl Barth stressed.[2] That Word, as the infinite Word of the Father, is beyond her and above her, even if the Father requires Mary in order to accomplish "the mystery of his purpose" for his Son and for us (Eph 1:9). In fact, only the Holy Spirit can incarnate the Word in Mary as both her Son and the Father's Son. Everything depends upon Jesus the infinite Word, as stands out in the seeming rebuff of Mary at Cana (Jn 2:4). Her "yes" becomes necessary since the God of the Covenant has already set up the pattern of dialogue and interpersonality.

The "first" incarnation of the Word in Mary is followed by a "second," as Mary lives and ponders the Word who now dwells substantially within her. St. Luke mentions the "second incarnation" twice in rapid succession: "As for Mary, she treasured all these things and pondered them in her heart" (Lk 2:19, 52).

---

2. Karl Barth, *Dogmatics in Outline*, London 1949, 90–91; see R. Laurentin, *A Year of Grace with Mary*, Dublin 1987, 82–83, where Laurentin expounds the thought of "the Church Father of the Reform."

Since Mary welcomed the Word and the Word became flesh in her, the Word had become at the same time the form of her life. Mary had stored this Word in her heart: wherever she would go, she is always seen in relation to this Word.... Mary is she — this is the way the Church sees Mary and for that reason calls her blessed — who has imprinted on herself the seal of the Word which she has given to us. It is fundamental that she became, so to speak, the emptiness that welcomed the Word of God (*Hohlform des Wortes*).[3]

Mariologists such as René Laurentin and Joseph Ratzinger had noticed the extent to which the Word of God in the first covenant had become flesh in Mary, the woman at the transition from the Old to the New, from the law to grace and truth (Jn 1:17; 2:4f), from the letter to the spirit, and from the Word to flesh.

Mary's "yes" at the annunciation, facilitating as it did the enfleshment of the eternal Word, launches Mary into the adventure of living by the Word and from the Word always and everywhere. For Mary to do so is for her to launch in turn a revolution of love, in fact, *the* revolution of love. The episodes in the Gospels, being like

---

3. Klaus Hemmerle, *Partire dall'unità*, 129–130.

a constellation of stars around Mary,[4] illustrate this "second" incarnation of the Word. Thus Luke's narrative of Mary's visitation to Elizabeth and Zachary dramatically parallels the two incarnations, as it were, with the consubstantial Word within Mary moving her to begin a revolution of love by living the words of Scripture concretely. An Irish theologian writes that

> in the visitation scene, we see that Mary is aware of the dimensions of what has happened.... This is the moment for Mary to tell her experience of what God has done in her life, "because she wants to give her light to everyone in the house." Her song, the *Magnificat* (Lk 1:46–55), tells of a revolution of love that has begun in her. Love has poured itself down upon earth, and it is Mary's lowliness and humility that lies at the heart of the "divine revolution" beginning among us.[5]

Christians "sing a new song to the Lord" (Ps 149:1). The reason is simple: "a new person sings a new song. A song is a thing of joy, and, if you think about it, also a thing of love. Those sing a new song who have discovered a new

---

4. Hans Urs von Balthasar, *Theo-drama*, III, San Francisco 1992, 299.

5. Brendan Leahy, *The Marian Profile in the Ecclesiology of Hans Urs von Balthasar*, New York 2000, 84.

life."[6] Now Mary is the human being who more than anyone else has discovered a new life, the life that has existed since the beginning, in fact, "the eternal life that was with the Father and was revealed to us" (1 Jn 1:2). It was understandable that her *Magnificat* should break forth after the in-breaking of absolute love into her whole person, body, soul and spirit. The *Magnificat* remains the song of the Church in praise of the God who is love.

As if to underline this translation of the second word into radical concrete action, Mary's *Magnificat* is simply studded with Old Testament texts and their echoes. The Word of God is so much the source and the texture of Mary's existence that it seems to mark and determine the very language and content of her speech. There is the eternal Word of the Father within, bone of her bone and flesh of her flesh, and the same Word is being translated into concrete living and practical action without. In one word, Mary is the woman wrapped in the Word.

The Holy Spirit had acted to incarnate the beloved Son in her as her Son. The same Holy Spirit, now "economically" the incarnate Son's rule of life, as it were, inspires Mary to

---

6. St. Augustine, *Sermo* 34, 1: CCL 41, 424.

live the Word of God continuously. A good
instance is John's account of the wedding feast
of Cana (2:1–11). There, Mary pre-empts the
impending embarrassment of the couple by
bringing it within the sphere of influence of her
Son. Her living-from-the-Word gives her eyes
for those around her, as well as the desire to put
them and their concrete needs into the heart of
the Son. Seemingly repulsed as prematurely
suggesting to her Son "his hour," Mary turns to
the organizers of the feast with the command
(the only one she gives in Scripture): "Do
whatever he tells you." Ignace de la Potterie
notices that this is the formula with which the
Mosaic Covenant is renewed.[7] For John, Mary
is therefore the woman who lives the covenant
by living the Words of the God of the Covenant.
Having first lived the living words of the living
God, she invites all others to do likewise. That is
the way by which the covenant-marriage of God
with humankind as sealed in the God-Man born
of Mary can become actual in time and space.

In St. John's perspective, however, Cana
finds its counterpoint on Calvary. On Calvary
the hour mentioned at Cana arrives. If at Cana
the miracle is the sign which "lets his glory
be seen" (2:11), on Calvary this glory shines

---

7. Ignace de la Potterie, *ibid.*, 188–190.

out for those who have the eyes to see, those, namely, who will "look upon him whom they have pierced" (19:37). The Fourth Gospel places Mary in the central tableau of the crucifixion narrative.[8]

A Double Piercing

At the foot of the Cross, Mary lives a two-fold piercing of soul as the hour of her Son's passion becomes the hour of her compassion. In the first instance, the sword of sorrow falls, piercing both the soul of the Man of Sorrows (Jn 19:34–36; Is 53:3; Lam 1:12) and the Mother's soul "so that the inner thoughts of many will be revealed" (Lk 1:35). St. Bernard of Clairvaux catches this first piercing poignantly.

> Blessed Mother, a sword did pierce your soul. For no sword could penetrate your Son's flesh without piercing your soul. The cruel lance, which opened his side and would not spare him in death though it could do him no injury, could not touch his soul. His soul was no longer there, but yours could not be set free, and it was pierced by a sword of sorrow.[9]

---

8. See Michael M. Mullins, *The Gospel of John. A Commentary*, Dublin 2003, 382–389.

9. St. Bernard, "The Sermons of St. Bernard," *Roman Breviary*, vol. III, 262–263.

What Bernard detects here is an abyss. The participation of the redeeming Son in human sorrow and suffering is met by Mary's unique participation in the Son's suffering as the *Desolata* standing under the Cross (Jn 19:25). Her unconditional assent to the incoming of the Son into her flesh thirty-three years previously "contained" this further "yes." But just as the first led to the birth of the Son into our history, so this second "yes" of Mary will be the occasion of a second birth when Mary will receive in the pain of her desolation a second motherhood, that of all believers: "Woman, behold your son" (Jn 19:27).

The second piercing of her soul consists in losing her Son. He appoints another in his own place when he nominates the beloved disciple as her new son representing the "new creation of a new humanity" (cf. Jn 19:26–7; 2 Cor 5:17; Gal 6:15). One cannot imagine a greater suffering for a mother, especially a mother like this. Not only does she lose her Son in the anguish of his dying and of his apparent abandonment by the Father, she also has to accept in his place a human substitute. This is the suffering of Mary's second motherhood, when she becomes mother of those reborn from and through the God-forsakenness of her Son.

Are we able to penetrate a little into the abyss of this second piercing and motherhood of the woman who is the mother of Jesus? Since the purpose of Jesus' coming and ministry, according to St. John, consists in "the gathering into unity of the scattered children of God" (Jn 11:52), it is to be expected that in the hour on Calvary, itself the summit of his whole ministry, he will form the family of the children of God. This is what John brings out in two masterly stokes. First, Jesus gives Mary to John as his Mother, and then John to Mary as her son. They constitute the first cell of the New Family, that new communion for which he prayed the previous night and for which he is now suffering to the end: "May they all be one, Father, as you and I are one" (Jn 17:21). As "the Church's foundation document,"[10] this appointment is a kind of first fruits of his prayer the previous evening in the Upper Room. "And from that moment the disciple took her to his own" (Jn 19:27).

In the second place, John goes on to tell of the piercing of the side of the dead Christ. He highlights the detail of the blood and the water that flowed out as the signs of the Eucharist and Baptism.[11] Perhaps the comments of St. John Chrysostom bring out the meaning best: "For as … God took a rib from Adam's side and formed

---

10. Hans Urs von Balthasar, *The Threefold Garland*, San Francisco 1982, 103.

11. See Mullins, *The Gospel of John*, 391–395.

woman, so Christ gave us blood and water from his side and formed the Church."[12] The Church is Woman, Mary in fact.[13] As such she lives the pain of "absolutely not being able to withdraw from the piercing of his side." She is with and in the New Adam, as the "New Eve," the favorite title believers gave her in the second and third centuries (1 Cor 15:45).[14] Her pain accompanies her "mothering of each new grace that does now reach our race."[15]

Mary, then, knows how to lose. She loses her Son willingly, if painfully. For since the annunciation at Nazareth, she has desired only one thing (Kierkegaard), fidelity to the will of God as expressed in the many words of God leading up through the Old Covenant to the consubstantial Word now become her Son. As at Nazareth she had to lose her plans in order to live the will of God her Savior, so here now on Calvary she also loses everything for her Son, except her love for him. In that love she accepts his mysterious design-blueprint for a new humankind, a communion of equal but distinct persons, participating in the

---

12. St. John Chrysostom, *Cat* 3:18, *Breviary*, Good Friday.

13. See Joseph Ratzinger, "Die Ekklesiologie der Konstitution *Lumen Gentium*," in *Weggemeinschaft des Glaubens*, Augsburg 2002, 129–131.

14. See John Henry Newman, *Letter to Pusey*, Westminister, Md. 1969, chap. 3, 26–76.

15. Hopkins, *ibid.*, 55.

eternal communion of the Three. The first "yes" made her the mother of the Son: the second "yes" will make her the mother of a multitude who are the members of her Son's new Body, the Church. As the closest collaborator with her Son in building the communion that is the Church, Mary becomes mysteriously his bride, the immaculate Bride-Church of the Lamb (Eph 5:25–27).

Four Marian Dogmas,
but One Communion of Life and Love

Catholic dogma has been one, whole, entire and sovereign from the beginning. It may not be added to, and one may not take away from it, without falling into *hairesis*, that ancient malady of picking and choosing which has perhaps returned in the guise of what is today called "menu Christianity." Of course Catholic dogma has grown and developed, not in itself but in our perception of it. This is hardly surprising if Catholic truth consists in the mystery of the Triune God of Love, the Persons who have communicated their own life and love to humanity and creation. The mystery can hardly be passed on (cf.1 Cor 11:23; 15:3) without the Church coming to understand it more deeply and unfolding its implications.

The major Marian dogmas make the point very well. These are Mary's divine motherhood as *Theotokos,* permanent virginity, immaculate conception, and assumption into the glory of her Son in the Trinity. These mysteries *fold out* from the one mystery-communion just described, and must always *fold back* into the same matrix. Of the three methods indicated in the First Vatican Council by which the "most fruitful understanding of the mysteries of faith" may be attained, the linking or "nexus" of the mysteries among themselves is the one that is most suited to our present interests.[16] We wish, in fact, to highlight Mary's witness to the communion that is the Church, the mystery that lies behind the Church, and the mission that lies before her.

The foundational Marian dogma is that of her divine motherhood.[17] Though the term, *Theotokos,* with its striking connotation as the "Begetter of God," was in use since around the middle of the third century, the doctrine was formally taught at the Third Ecumenical Council held at Ephesus in A.D. 431. Now what is striking is that Ephesus was not called in the first instance to touch Mariology at all. It was called to address a heresy attacking Christ, the heresy of Nestorius, Patriarch of Constantinople.

---

16. First Vatican Council, *Dogmatic Constitution on the Catholic Faith,* DS 3016.

17. For the text of the Council of Ephesus, see Norman P. Tanner, S.J., *Decrees of the Ecumenical Councils,* volume I, London and Washington, D.C., 1990, 58f.

Nestorius' difficulties had to do with his Christology; that is, not directly with Mary but with Mary's Son. They led him to reject two statements widely current at the time: "One of the Trinity was crucified on the cross," and "Mary is Mother of God" — Nestorius preferred to call her "the Mother of Christ."

Thus Nestorius saw in Christ *two* sons, an eternal Son of the Father and a human son of Mary, these forming nothing but a "moral unity." The Christ of Nestorius was therefore a kind of "split personality." Effectively Nestorius wanted the divine Son to keep his distance from humanity, not throw in his lot utterly with human flesh and the human condition. This was an assault on the very thing that makes Christian faith unique, and human life into a divine adventure. It tried to separate what God has united in the wonder of the incarnation. It seems that, for Nestorius, Jesus the man was willing to give up his life for us, but the Son of the Father was not (perhaps because he ought not)!

Led by Cyril of Alexandria, the Council taught that "the Word from God the Father has been united by hypostasis with the flesh and is one Christ with his own flesh, and is therefore God and man together." There is a "hypostatic union" between God and man. This means that the Person of the Son (the second

Person of the blessed Trinity) "hypostatized" or "personalized" the humanity he received from Mary. The body and soul of Jesus are human, but the Person to whom they belong is not a human person. He is rather the divine Son of the divine Father. Thus we have access to the Father through Christ, and in no other way, as the Gospels repeatedly teach (Jn 14:6b). The Word's personalizing of the humanity taken from Mary means that "we are in Christ as one mystical person," and Christ is head of the whole human family.[18]

To preserve this teaching, the Council had to affirm that Mary is *Theotokos*. The title asserts that her Son is God, it insists on his genuine humanity, and suggests the mode of the union between both. Earlier heretics had said that her Son was not God, as Arius did before the Council of Nicaea in 325, or that he was not truly man, as Apollinarius did before Constantinople I in 381. Now the Council had to defend against Nestorius the unity of both God and man in the one Person of Jesus of Nazareth. Thus all the heresies that attacked the Son tended in God's most wise providence to exalt the Mother, whose new glory in the Church was to reverse the humility of her station during previous

---

18. St. Thomas, *Summa*, III, q. 48, a. 2, ad 1; *De Veritate*, I, q.29, a. 4; see St. Bernard, *In Laudibus Virginis Matris*, Homily IV, 8.

centuries.[19] Only this elevation of Mary would safeguard the full depth and truth of the incarnation.

Just as Mary once sheltered and protected the Christ-child from the designs of Herod, so now she sheltered him from the designs of heretics. The doctrine of Mary's divine maternity, in fact, protects and highlights the mysterious union-communion set up by Christ in his incarnation, when God out of love becomes what we are so that we can become by grace what he is. Mary is the great protagonist of this communion, not only existentially (as we have been considering) but also ontologically.

19. John Henry Newman, *Discourses to Mixed Congregations*, London 1921, 346–349, 357.

Chapter III

Mary in the Mission of the Church:
The "Claritas" and Radiance of Love

God the Holy Trinity, the mystery of all mysteries, freely chose to create a world of free and intelligent human beings made in his image and likeness. We were all chosen in Christ since before the creation of the world (Eph 1:4). From all eternity, the Father had this special project in his heart: to create men and women as sons and daughters in his eternally begotten Son and in the freedom and communion of the Holy Spirit. This is why in the early Church each person was seen as a unique "word" in the eternal Word, and all of us together as "words in the Word." The design of God is one of divine generosity, for, as the early Fathers of the Church clearly saw, "goodness loves to scatter itself."

In that perspective the New Adam (cf. 1 Cor 15) and the New Eve are unique, since they are the progenitors of a new humanity that lives now from the life of the eternal Trinity, in training for future blessedness, and, though having to bear for a time all kinds of sufferings (2 Cor 11:22–28), in a joy that "no eye has seen, nor ear heard, nor the heart of any person ever imagined" (1 Cor 2:8). This new humanity consists of persons who when they participate in the life of God will come to know the eternal Persons even as they have been known (1 Cor 13:12). In that way, they will advance from one state of glory to another (2 Cor 3:18).

In the wonder of divine revelation, the life of the Blessed Trinity is communicated and mediated to humankind by the Son and the Holy Spirit as the form of our life with the Trinity. In that mediation, the mother of Jesus exemplifies the role of the creature in the co-redemption of creatures. "This participation in the work of salvation has been elevated into the Mariological mystery,"[1] writes the great Lutheran philosopher, Eric Voegelin. One begins to notice how many may participate in the same mystery. Mystery, in other words, becomes communion. The Church is this communion as "a people made one from the unity of the Father, the Son and the Holy Spirit." In the divine-human communion Mary as the Second Eve occupies a place second only to that of her Son. She receives a mission corresponding to her dramatic "appointment" on Calvary as mother of those born from the pierced side of the New Adam while he slept the sleep of death on the Cross (Jn 17:27). Placed in the *mystery* from the beginning, embedded in the *communion* that flows from that mystery, Mary also receives a *mission* whose dimensions are now dawning on the Church and humankind.

---

1. Eric Voegelin, Letter to Alfred Schutz "On Christianity," in Peter J. Opitz and Gregor Sebba, editors, *The Philosophy of Order. Essays on History, Consciousness and Politics*, Stuttgart 1981, 449–457: here at 455.

Our reflections to date on divine revelation have thrown up a law that is operative in all the works of God: *to love is to make the beloved important*. To be convinced of this it is enough to think of the joy of parents upon the achievement of their children, or, to change the example, witness the joy of teachers upon the performance of diligent students, or of a coach in sports upon the victory of the team he has guided and motivated. All these instances serve to highlight the joy of the lover over the achievement of the beloved. If we created human persons put forward those we love, highlighting their achievements and rejoicing with them in their success, how much more would the Divine Persons put forward this singular creature of their Grace!

The truth is that the very events of divine revelation illustrate this law abundantly. Each one of the divine Persons "exalts" the Others. Could they stop doing this when the Son becomes flesh and the Holy Spirit is sent? That would be impossible. The Gospels in fact show us clearly what happens. The Father loving the Son puts him forward as the one we should welcome: "This is my Son, the Chosen One. Listen to him" (Lk 9:35). The Son, however, puts forward the Father: "The world must know that I love the Father" (Jn 14:31). The Holy Spirit as the bond of love-communion between the Father and the Son puts both forward! At the Last Supper, Jesus stresses this fact to the Twelve, "The Holy Spirit will glorify me since all he tells you will be taken from what is mine" (Jn 16:14), and, "The Spirit cries *Abba! Father!*" (Gal 4:6; Rom 8:15). This law is but the expression in history and in our world of the life of mutual indwelling (*perichoresis*) among the divine Persons in the transcendent Trinity.

Will this law cease to function when it comes to the place of creatures in the mystery-communion of the Church? Mary of Nazareth, the Mother of the Lord (Lk 1:43), provides the most unequivocal answer possible. He who is mighty does great things for her. He calls her to be the Mother of his co-eternal and only begotten Son (Lk 1:26–38). He answers her question as to how such a wonder might happen by promising her the overshadowing of the Holy Spirit (Lk 1:35), who in her will effect the indwelling of his eternal Son become her child. In a certain sense, all the three Persons have worked together to exalt this creature. Indeed, to love is to make the other important, and to love Mary is to exalt her. All ages will call her blessed (Lk 1:48), as they perceive what the Holy Trinity has done for, in and through her.

The Fathers of the Church compared Christ with the sun in the sky, Mary with the moon as the reflected glory of Christ, and the martyrs with the more distant stars in the heavens. In the incarnation, however, all this is inverted, as it were. Because now God has emptied himself (Phil 2:7-8), made himself small before this creature whom he will call by the sweet name of mother. She is the woman whom God the Holy Trinity loves uniquely, and in whom They love the whole of creation. A modern mystic and founder puts the point with great punch and power, "In the past we had seen Mary in relation to Christ and the saints — to make a comparison — as in the heavens where there is the moon (Mary) in relation to the sun (Christ) and the stars (the saints). Now, it was no longer so. The Mother of God embraced, like a vast blue sky, the sun itself, God himself.... We had contemplated Mary as being set within the Trinity, but now, because of her Son, in her own particular way, we saw her as containing the Trinity."[2]

And there is more. In the moment when the eternal Son concludes his mission on the hill of Calvary and pours forth the Holy Spirit (Jn 19:30), the hour in fact where his glory shines out through the depths of his self-emptying love for us (Phil 2:6-8), he names Mary as the Mother of his disciples, as we have seen. In the new hu-

---

2. Chiara Lubich, *Mary. The Transparency of God*, London and New York 2003, 26.

manity being born from the love of the eternal Son lived "to the end" (Jn 13:1), Mary receives her mission of "second motherhood." She who had put the Father and his Son and their Holy Spirit forward in such incomparable fashion at Nazareth, renewing that option radically at Cana and proposing it to others (Jn 2:5), now receives the mission of a motherhood set into the communion of the Church. The Son puts her forward to the point of appointing her Mother of all the redeemed.[3]

What will be Mary's attitude before this great mission? Just as she was utterly available both at Nazareth and on Calvary, at the cost of the sword and the cross, so from now on in the historical pilgrimage of the Church Mary will put forward the God and Father of her Son. She will also put forward all her new children, seeing in them the replicas-to-be of her Son, the children of the Father and the temples of the Holy Spirit. Hers will be the agenda of her Son, the laws of his Kingdom and the imperatives of the Sermon on the Mount. Had she not already sung in her *Magnificat*, with all the fire of the prophets, "The Lord has brought down the powerful from their thrones, and lifted up the lowly; he has filled the hungry with good things, and sent the rich away

---

3. See Oliver Treanor, *Mother of the Redeemer*, Dublin 1988.

empty" (Lk 1:52–3)? Mary is liberation theology.

As an authentic "nothingness of love," Mary entirely serves the communion formed by God the Holy Trinity. She desires only one thing: that her Son "christen" humankind ever more fully as the centuries succeed one another, and that all generations be drawn into his mystery. As the time of the Church unfolds, the place of the Mother of God will unfold in ever-greater clarity: she whose very existence consists in putting others forward cannot be hidden for long. History, in fact, has shown how "she has grown into her place in the Church by a tranquil influence and a natural process."[4]

---

4. John Henry Newman, *Discourses to Mixed Congregations*, 357; see also his *Sermons on Subjects of the Day*, London 1871, 36–37.

Conclusion

M ary, then, is an incomparable witness to "the faith given once for all to the saints" (Jude 3). In her the destinies of the world are reversed. It is for this reason that the Second Vatican Council teaches that "Mary, in a way, unites in her person and re-echoes the most important doctrines of the faith."[1] Her biblical portrait throws light on "the mystery of our religion" (1 Tim 3:16) as a threefold revelation of mystery, communion and mission. In her and through her we see the world's "re-creation" by the Son of God and the Holy Spirit, acting as the two "arms" of the Father. In that way she enables us to perceive how "the Church is a people made one from the unity of the Father, the Son and the Holy Spirit." Thus, she enables us to grasp what Vatican II stressed in its opening chapter appropriately headed, "The Mystery of the Church."

She illuminates the communion of the Church that flows from the creating and re-creating God. In particular, the great truths concerning her place in the communion bring out the proportion and harmony of the whole communion. Finally, by her witness of the love with which she loved divine Love she inspires the mission of the Church on earth, even as she employs the weapon of prayer in heaven on its

---

1. *Lumen Gentium*, 65.

behalf. In the visit to her cousin, Elizabeth, love drives her to tell her experience of the mystery she carries in her womb. However, she tells it first by deeds and only then in the words of her *Magnificat*. St. Ambrose, the fourth-century Father of the Church, seems to capture this truth when he comments on Mary's visitation of Elizabeth. "Joyful in her promise, dedicated in her task, quick in her joy, Mary hurried into the hill country."[2] Mary first tells by deeds of love and later by the words of love of her *Magnificat*. She believes that love is stronger than selfishness, in fact, that it is the only reality that can change human hearts. This makes her the bright star of evangelization, since she radiates the reflected glory of "the Lord of glory" (1 Cor 2:8). This means that the Mother of Jesus points to the fullness, the proportion and the *claritas* of the divine revelation that lives in the Church for the life of the world and the glory of the God of Jesus Christ.

Fullness, proportion and radiance, however, are also the very components of beauty. This is the insight of St. Thomas Aquinas, who summarizes the great tradition of pagan antiquity and the early Church.[3] We have seen the manner in

---

2. St. Ambrose, *Commentary on the Gospel of Luke*, Book II, 19: CCL 14, 39.

3. St. Thomas, *Summa*, I, q. 39, a. 8.

which Mary highlights these dimensions of the mystery of faith, letting the glory-beauty of Christ "from her flow off, and no way but so" (Hopkins). In her we see the fullness of the mystery, the proportion and harmony of the communion that is the Church, and the radiance of the love exalted by God-Love in order to radiate the *claritas* of that love into the world. She is therefore "the Mother of Fair Love," and from her shines the beauty of the faith and life that will in fact save the world.

> I am the Mother of beautiful love, of fear, of knowledge, and of holy hope.
>
> Ecclesiasticus 24:18 (NRSV)

Afterword

The Blessed Virgin, the Lady in whom divinity rhymes with humanity, is both Maiden and Mother. The image of Our Lady of Guadalupe, Patroness of the Americas, shows a young woman heavy with child. What exactly is this unique motherhood that was of such paramount importance to the imagination of Christians? What mystery does it still represent for us, in an age of surrogate mothers, broken families, teenage pregnancies and — in a few years — artificial wombs and human clones?

In the fourth century, Saint Ephrem sings of the Nativity:

No one quite knows, Lord, what to call
your mother: should we call her "virgin"?
— but her giving birth is an established fact;
or "married woman"?
— but no man has known her.
If your mother's case is beyond
   comprehension,
who can hope to understand yours?

She alone is your mother,
but she is your sister with everyone else.
She was your mother, she was your sister,
she was your bride too
along with all chaste souls.
You, who are your mother's beauty,
yourself adorned her with everything!

She was, by her nature, your bride already
before you came; she conceived in a manner
quite beyond nature after you had come,
O Holy One, and was a virgin
when she gave birth to you in most
    holy fashion.

With you Mary underwent all that married
    women undergo;
conception — but without intercourse;
her breast filled with milk — but against
    nature's pattern:
you made her, the thirsty earth,
all of a sudden into a fountain of milk.

If she could carry you, it was because you,
    the great Mountain
had lightened your weight;
if she feeds you, it is because you had taken
    on hunger;
if she gives you her breast, it is because you
of your own will, had thirsted;
if she fondles you, you, who are the fiery
    coal of mercy,
preserved her bosom unharmed.

Your mother is a cause for wonder:
the Lord entered into her and became
    a servant;
he who is the Word entered — and became
    silent within her;

thunder entered her — and made no sound;
there entered the Shepherd of all,
and in her he became the Lamb,
bleating as he comes forth.[1]

This conception and birth, quite "beyond nature" as St. Ephrem says, are not "sub-natural" like some postmodern genetic experiment, but *supernatural*. By that we mean "more natural than natural." This is a glimpse of what nature was meant to be, and what it can be again if soaked and penetrated by divine grace. Mary is not the alien, not the unnatural one — we are. As for her purity, does that make her more remote from us, or closer, because able to come to us without fear or jealousy or hatred or selfishness?

Is it not wonderful that Our Lady is able to pray to her God with him on her lap, or in her womb? Is it possible to say that by making himself our Eucharist, by inviting us to receive him into our bodies in Holy Communion, her Son is trying to achieve something of the same intimacy with us?

So many of the beautiful statues that one may visit in Marian shrines emphasize by the position of his feet, the position of her hands, in a language of gesture and posture the mystery of the Incarnation which created a bridge between

---

1. Extracted from "Hymns on the Nativity," no. 11, in *The Harp of the Spirit*, trans. Sebastian Brock, Oxford 1983.

heaven and earth, human and divine nature. The Mother is the matrix, the world that the Child grows up in; she is his *planet*. Her earthiness, her role as living symbol of the dark and fertile soil of creation, as the ground of our humanity and our beseeching, is probably represented best in the Black Madonnas that some misguided feminists have tried to claim for the Earth Goddess.

Was Henry Adams right, that Mary was more real to the people of the Middle Ages than her Son? And was it right that she should be? He tells the tale of a clerk who never stopped repeating the Ave Maria, until at last the Lord appeared to him and said, "My Mother thanks you much for all the Salutations that you make her; but still you should not forget to salute me also."

Whatever the rightness of the balance between Mother and Son in the devotions of the Middle Ages, the fact is that they are inseparable in time and in eternity. It is from her body alone that he takes his human nature. However far he travels from her side as an adult, she is for ever the center of his world because she is his point of origin, and when he is laid in her lap as a corpse — and in the tomb that is again the symbol of her womb, ready for the Resurrection — she is the heart of the world that he has come to save and to transform. She is the heart of the world, she is the ground of our humanity, she is the "air we breathe," and so much else (the Holy Grail, the Ark of the Covenant, the Burning Bush), but she is more than merely a symbol of these things. She is an archetype in the Christian imagination, but she is more than an archetype, as her Son is also more than an archetype. She is a *person*. As a sinless person, she more *real* and solid as a person than any fallen creature can quite conceive. She is a person, and to be a person — according to Hans Urs von Balthasar and Adrienne von Speyr — is to have a mission, to *be* a mission. Her mission, her task, her freely chosen identity, is to be the Mother of God. God takes her willingness and magnifies it by pouring his grace into it.

The mystery of Mary, then, is the mystery of motherhood — of parenthood, human and divine. This is the mystery of the Church, the mystery of salvation which is something to do with re-creation, with "renewing the face of the earth" and giving birth to the "people" (the Church or *Ecclesia*) that is also the Body of Christ. It is the mystery of divine Wisdom, of creation and re-creation. This wisdom unfolds in the relationship between Mother and Child. It is a wisdom that we too seek in our meditations here, with this booklet: in prayer, poetry, and theology.

Léonie Caldecott

Glossary

Anathema, anathematization — meaning to curse or reject, it is used in connection with decisions taken by the Church (for example in an Ecumenical Council) to reject a particular doctrine or idea as untrue, misleading or heretical.

Annunciation, the — the "announcement" to Mary by the angel that she had been chosen to be mother of the Messiah (Luke 1:26–38).

Assumption, assumed — to assume is to "take up," so the word is used in theology to refer to the taking up of human nature by the Person of the Son in the hypostatic union, as well as to the bodily "taking up" of the Blessed Virgin Mary into heaven at the end of her earthly life, as defined by Pope Pius XII in 1950.

Calvary — the hill outside Jerusalem where Jesus Christ was crucified, sometimes used to refer to the whole experience of crucifixion.

Communion, Holy Communion — since a "communion" is a union of several or many people in one "body," united by a common spirit of love, it is applied in a special sense to reception of the Eucharist or Blessed Sacrament, by which the members of the Church are united into the Body of Christ.

Consubstantial — "of one substance with"; used first at the Council of Nicaea in 325 to affirm the equality of the Son with the Father. The divine nature is a single undivided "substance" though the Persons that share that nature are three (Father, Son, and Holy Spirit).

Covenant, Mosaic covenant — a covenant is a "coming together" in the strong sense of an agreement that establishes a permanent bond between the partners. It is applied to the relationship established by God with Abraham and his descendants, including Moses (the "Mosaic covenant"), and renewed in Jesus Christ (the "New Covenant" or "New Testament").

Dabar — Hebrew for "Word" or "Act," first used in Gen. 15, equivalent to Greek "Logos."

Dogma, Marian dogma — an authoritative doctrine taught by the Church, in the case of "Marian" dogmas those concerning the Blessed Virgin Mary (especially her perpetual virginity, her immaculate conception, and her assumption into heaven).

Ecumenical Councils — General Councils of the bishops of the Church beginning with the Council of Nicaea in 325, especially the first seven which are recognized by both Catholic and Orthodox, but understood by Catholics as including many others, right up to the First and Second Vatican Councils in the 19th and 20th centuries respectively.

Eucharist — literally "thanksgiving," it refers to the Mass in which the Last Supper and Passion of the Lord is commemorated and made present, as well as to the Blessed Sacrament of the Lord's body and blood which is offered and received in the Mass.

Existential — that which has to do with human existence and life.

Grace — the good will, favor or assistance of God.

Hypostasis, hypostatically, hypostatic union — literally (in Greek) "that which stands beneath," or "underlying reality," hypostasis was adapted to refer not to "substance" (the equivalent word in Latin, for which there was also the word ousia in Greek) but to "person," in order to be able to express the fact that Christ is both God and man. The union of divine and human natures in Christ in one hypostasis or persona was termed "hypostatic union" at the Council of Chalcedon in 451.

Incarnation, the — the assumption of human nature (body and soul) by the Second Person of the Blessed Trinity.

Intercession — prayer on behalf of another.

Kyrios — "Lord": the title given to the Jesus upon his resurrection (Phil 2:11).

Magnificat, the – Mary's song of praise and gratitude for the favors shown to her by God, as recorded in Luke 1:46–55.

Mariology — the orderly theological study of the Blessed Virgin Mary (to be distinguished from "Mariolatry", the worship of Mary, which is rejected by the Church).

Messiah — the Anointed One or "Christ," the prophesied future king and savior of Israel.

Ontological — having to do with being or reality, as opposed to the merely notional or logical.

Paschal Mystery — the mystery of Easter, i.e., the death and resurrection of Christ, derived from the Hebrew and Aramaic word for Passover.

Perichoresis — Greek term used to describe the mutual love and indwelling of the Father, the Son, and the Holy Spirit (cf. Jn 14:11).

Person — originally persona (Latin) or prosopon (Greek), referring to the mask worn by a classical actor to signify the characters he played, it was adopted by the Church Fathers as the Latin equivalent of hypostasis, used to refer to God the Father, Son or Holy Spirit rather than to God in general. From there it came to be applied to human individuals understood as existing in relation to God and to each other.

Post-exilic — referring to the time after the Exile of the Hebrew people to Babylon in the sixth century before Christ. (Exile is not to be confused with "Exodus," the much earlier liberation from Egypt under Moses in the thirteenth century, B.C.)

Redeemed, redemption, Co-redemptrix — to redeem is to buy back or ransom, and since Christ's death was the price he paid to recover us from the Evil One he is known as our Redeemer. Some theologians speak of the Virgin Mary as the "Co-redemptrix" because she co-operated with the "one Mediator between God and man" (1 Tim 2:5) in this work.

Revelation — the religion which God communicated to humanity by his manifestation to Israel and supremely by his self-communication in his Son, Jesus Christ.

Runai De — lit. the "secretary" or "secrets-keeper" of God (Gaelic). Ancient title given to Mary in relation to Christ, who is the eternal "secret" of the Father (Col 1:26).

Salvation, Savior — in Christian terms, salvation is from the consequences of the Fall, namely the death and suffering of the soul, and the one Savior who can bring this about is Jesus Christ, by virtue of his sacrifice on the Cross.

Synergy, synergically — the word means "working together" or combining forces.

Theotokos — "God-bearer". The title was given to Mary by the Third Ecumenical Council assembled at Ephesus in 431.

Trinity, Economic and Transcendent — the Father, the Son, and the Holy Spirit: one God, three persons. The Economic is the Trinity as revealed to us in the missions of Christ and of the Holy Spirit; the Transcendent is the Trinity existing in heaven, outside or beyond time (sometimes called the "Immanent Trinity").

Unmoved Mover — the name which the Greek philosopher, Aristotle (b. 387) gave to God as the First Cause of all reality.

Word, the — the English translation of the Greek "Logos" used in John's Gospel to refer to the eternal Son of the divine Father.

Zion — the sacred mountain or City of David, also used to refer to Israel and its capital Jerusalem.

Select Bibliography

A.M. Allchin, *The Joy of all Creation* (London: New City, 1984).

Hans Urs von Balthasar and Joseph Cardinal Ratzinger, *Mary: The Church at the Source*, trans. Adrian Walker (San Francisco: Ignatius Press, 2005).

Ignace de la Potterie, S.J., *Mary in the Mystery of the Covenant* (New York: St Paul's, 1992).

Andre Feuillet, *Jesus and His Mother: The Role of the Virgin Mary in Salvation History and the Place of Woman in the Church*, trans. Leonard Maluf (Still River, MA: St Bede's Publications, 1984).

Luigi Gambero, *Mary in the Fathers* (San Francisco: Ignatius Press, 1999).

Jean Guitton, *The Blessed Virgin* (London: Burns Oates, 1952).

John Paul II, Pope, *Mulieris Dignitatem* [On the Dignity and Vocation of Women], Vatican City, 2002.

John Paul II, Pope, *Redemptoris Mater* [Mother of the Redeemer], Vatican City, 1987.

Brendan Leahy, *The Marian Profile in the Ecclesiology of Hans Urs von Balthasar* (New York: New City Press, 2000).

Chiara Lubich, *Essential Writings: Spirituality, Dialogue, Culture* (London and New York: New City Press, 2007).

Chiara Lubich, *Mary: The Transparency of God* (London and New York: New City Press, 2003).

M. M. Miles (ed.), *Maiden and Mother: Prayers, Hymns, Songs and Devotions to Honor the Blessed Virgin Mary* (London: Burns Oates, 2001).

John Henry Newman, *"Letter to Pusey,"* in Difficulties of Anglicans, Vol. 2 (London: Longmans, Green & Co., 1881).

Maire O'Byrne, *Model of Incarnate Love. Mary Desolate in the Experience and Thought of Chiara Lubich* (New York: New City Press, 2011).

Michael O'Carroll, CSSP, *Theotokos: An Encyclopedia on the Blessed Virgin Mary* (Collegeville, MN: Liturgical Press, 1990).

Joseph Ratzinger, *Daughter Zion* (San Francisco: Ignatius Press, 1987).

Adrienne von Speyr, *Handmaid of the Lord*, trans. E.A. Nelson (San Francisco: Ignatius Press, 1985).

Adrienne von Speyr, *Mary in the Redemption*, trans. Helena M. Tomko (San Francisco: Ignatius Press, 2003).